To... e
Lost Girl

by
Ryan Chase

GLOBE FEARON
Pearson Learning Group

Project Editor: Brian Hawkes
Editorial Assistants: Jennifer Keezer, Jenna Thorsland
Editorial Development: ELHI Publishers, LLC
Art Supervision: Sharon Ferguson
Production Editor: Regina McAloney
Electronic Page Production: Debbie Childers
Manufacturing Supervisor: Mark Cirillo
Cover Design: Sharon Ferguson
Illustrator: Steven Cavallo

ISBN 0-130-23291-2
Printed in the United States of America

4 5 6 7 8 9 10 11   05 04 03 02

Globe
Fearon

Pearson Learning Group

1-800-321-3106
www.pearsonlearning.com

Contents

1. The Play's the Thing 5

2. Tryouts 8

3. Girl Problems 11

4. No Time to "Take 10" 13

5. Fired Up 16

6. Who's Driving Donna? 20

7. On the QT 22

8. Put Off the Play? No Way! 25

9. What About Donna? 29

10. Cleaning Up 32

11. Kay Is Next 35

12. The Lost Girl. 38

13. Getting It Out. 41

14. Tonight's the Night 44

1. The Play's the Thing

"OK, class. That is it for today," says Mrs. Newman. "I need your schoolwork back to me in one week."

"A week?" says Tom. "Can't we have a little longer?"

"Sorry," says Mrs. Newman. "One week. I wanted to give you a little more time, but we have the play coming up too."

"Play!" the kids say. "What play?"

"Principal Walls wants to put on a Mountain School play," she says. "And with the talking that goes on in **my** class," Mrs. Newman laughs, "I just **know** a lot of you will want to be in it!"

"Are you saying we talk a lot?" says Kay.

"I'll put it this way, Kay," says Mrs. Newman.

"Do you know anyone in my class who has to come in after school for talking too little?"

The kids laugh. "You have us there, Mrs. Newman," says Kay.

"What about the play?" says Jared. "What can we do to get in it?"

"Principal Walls and I are having tryouts on Saturday," she says. "Anyone who wants to be in the play needs to be at the school by 9:00 A.M."

"By 9:00 A.M.?" says Donna. "On my day to sleep in? Ooo, no!"

"I'm sorry," laughs Mrs. Newman, "but I just know you can make it! Think of it as a — as a race, Donna," she laughs. "A race for a new 'do' at the Inwear-Out Shop!"

"OK, OK," says Donna. "I'll try."

"Way to go, Mrs. Newman!" says Jared. "That is how to get Donna going. Just say 'NEW' and 'INWEAR-OUT SHOP'!" His friendly kidding gets the class laughing and talking.

"Time is up, kids!" says Mrs. Newman over the talking. "Don't forget about the tryouts because I want to see a lot of you there!"

Tom, Jared, Kay, Donna, and the class get up to go. Then Dan Ringover walks up to Jared. "Are you laughing at my girl?" he says. Dan and Donna have been going out.

"About Saturday?" Jared says. "No, man, I'm just kidding her."

Donna walks over to Dan and Jared. "It's OK, Jared, I know you are kidding. Dan, don't make problems," she says. Dan gives Jared another look, then he and Donna walk out. Donna looks back to say she is sorry, but then goes with Dan.

"What was that about?" Tom says.

"You got me," says Jared as he gets his backpack. "But he didn't look happy."

2. Tryouts

The kids have a problem waiting for Saturday, because they want to know about the big play. That day Jared, Tom, Kay, Donna, and the others get to school at 9:00.

"I see we are up and at it," says Kay.

"I, for one, feel like a truck hit me," says Donna, "but I **did** make it on time."

They see Principal Walls in the hall. "Just the kids I want to see!" the principal says. "Come with me." They go into a class where Mrs. Newman is waiting and wait just a little longer for other kids to come. After a little time goes by, Mrs. Newman talks about the play.

"This is a play about a painter who wants to make people happy with his work," says Principal Walls.

"A girl sees him painting day after day and goes out of her way to walk by to see how his work is going. She does not look happy, and the painter wants to make her laugh."

The principal goes on, "She and the painter get to be friends. But then it gets cold out, and she no longer comes. The painter does not know where the girl is, or what to do to go about finding her. He thinks she does not have a home, and may be cold. What will she do? How will she hold on?"

The kids like the play and can't wait to try out for parts. There is a shopkeeper, a cop, and a teller at a bank, but the big parts are the painter and the Lost Girl. One by one, Principal Walls and Mrs. Newman work with the kids to see who will play which part.

After they try out, Principal Walls and Mrs. Newman go into a class to talk it over. The kids wait.

"Who do you think they will find for the Painter?" says Tom.

"I don't think I will get the part of the Lost Girl," says Donna.

"Maybe," Kay says, "but **I'm** the one who didn't know what to say!"

"What about you, Jared?" Donna says. "How did you do?"

"A bad job, for the most part," says Jared, "so it looks like the Painter may go to anyone."

They wait and wait for the principal and Mrs. Newman to come back out. Then the big news: "Kids, Mrs. Newman and I have made Jared our Painter, and Kay the Lost Girl. Donna is the bank teller, Jake is the shopkeeper, and Tom is the cop."

Kay is so happy she screams. Donna did want to be the Lost Girl, but she is happy for Kay. Jared, Tom, and Jake are laughing.

"We will work on the play in school," Mrs. Newman says. "And the people who did not get **in** it will help work **on** it — doing painting, woodworking, and the like."

Principal Walls walks the kids out, saying, "We will make *The Lost Girl* a play that Mountain School will not forget!"

3. Girl Problems

The kids are laughing and happy as they come from tryouts. It is by the back hall that Tom sees Dan Ringover waiting for Donna.

"Donna," Tom says, "Dan is over there waiting for you."

Donna looks over at Dan, then back to Tom. "You and the others can go on," she says. "I'll see you at school next week."

Tom sees Donna go over to Dan, and she tells him about the tryouts. Dan looks a little mad. Jared, who is waiting by Tom, sees Tom looking at Donna. "You have it bad for her, don't you?" Jared says.

"I like Donna a lot," says Tom, "but she doesn't know I'm alive."

"Then tell her," Jared says.

"No, I don't think I can," Tom says. "She is going out with Ringover. It will just have to wait."

"OK, Tom," says Jared. "But she can't go out with you if she doesn't know you like her."

"Ssshhhh," says Tom as Kay and Jake come over.

Kay hears him. "OK, what's up?" she says.

"Not a lot," says Tom.

"Out with it, out with it," Kay says. "I want to know."

"And I don't want to tell," says Tom.

"Come on, Tom," Kay and Jake say. "We are your friends! You can tell us!"

"You just don't give up, do you?" says Tom. "OK, people, that is it. I'm out of here," Tom says, walking out of the hall. "See you," he calls out.

"What's with him?" Kay wants to know.

"Just a little girl problem," Jared says.

"No, no, that can't be it," says Jake, laughing.

"Why?" Jared says.

"E-Z," laughs Jake, "because there are no **little** girl problems, my man. Just **big** ones!"

4. No Time to "Take 10"

The weeks go by fast as the kids work with Mrs. Newman and Principal Walls on the play.

"Tom, I think we are going to need to lighten up the paint on that wooden shelter," says Mrs. Newman one day as they work in class.

"OK, Mrs. Newman," says Tom. "Painters!" he calls out. "Where are the painters?"

"Cleaning up," Kay says. "They will be back."

"What about the houselights?" Jared says. "Did anyone have time to look and see if they work?"

"I did!" says Jake. "And they do — which makes that one problem out, with about 500 to go!" he laughs. "By the way," he says as Jared walks away, "Kay and I are getting out *The Lost Girl* ad, too, which makes it just 499 problems to go."

"I need **0** problems," Jared laughs.

"I think what we need is to stop all this work and take 10!" says Mrs. Newman.

"You don't have to tell me that more than one time!" says Jared. He and Tom go out in the hall, where they talk with the others.

"This is going to be a hit!" Kay says. "I just know it!"

"Looks that way," Tom says. "We just have to wait for Saturday night to see if other people think so."

"Are you scared?" he says to Kay and Jared.

"Not me," says Jared.

"A little," says Kay.

Donna walks over to her friends. "You don't need to be scared," she tells them. "You and Jared know your parts!"

"I'm just happy that Principal Walls had you and Tom back us up on our parts," says Kay. "That way, if Jared or I get sick, you can take over."

"No problem," says Donna. "But you will not get sick, Kay."

Jared looks back and sees Dan Ringover waiting for Donna. "Dan," he says, "don't hide over there. Come on over and help out."

"I'm not hiding," says Dan, "and I have other work I need to do. I'm just looking in on Donna." Dan gives Jared a long look. "Is that a problem?"

No one talks. Jared does not know what to say. Then Donna says, "No, it's not a problem, Dan. We just have more painting and cleaning to do here." She stops. "Tell you what," she says. "How about if I call you at home, OK?" Dan doesn't look too happy, but he goes out to his car.

"I think your boyfriend has a problem," Tom says to Donna.

"In a way," says Donna. "He wanted me to be the Lost Girl in the play."

"You're kidding," says Tom. "It's just a play, not a job for all time! Anyway," he says, "you **did** get to be the bank teller."

"I know," says Donna, "and **I'm** happy. It's Dan who is not."

"What about his 'looking in' on you? Does he do that a lot?" Tom says.

"More than I like," laughs Donna. "He wants me with him 100% of the time."

Who doesn't? thinks Tom.

5. Fired Up

Jared, Tom, and Kay walk out of the school, hot after another long day of working on the play.

"Ooo, it's snowing!" Kay screams, and races off to make a snowball.

"That's new in the mountains?" laughs Jared.

"It's new today!" says Kay.

"I'm with her," says Tom, making snowballs with his friend. "After all that work, the cold and the snow feel OK."

"1–2–3–GO!" say Tom and Kay, hitting Jared with snowballs.

"AAAAAAAH!" Jared calls out.

"With friends like us," laughs Tom, looking at the snow on Jared, "you may be **wearing** snow home!"

"If you care to know," laughs Jared, getting the snow off, "I want dinner, not snowballs."

"OK, OK," says Kay. "If you are going to be that way, Jared, then I'll help you up and you can drive me home!"

"Why do I feel like I just lost?" kids Jared.

"Because you did!" Kay kids back. "Come on."

Tom sees Jared and Kay go, then sees Donna walk out of the school.

"Donna," he calls. "Do you need me to drive you home?"

Donna looks over the lots in back of the school, but she doesn't see Dan.

"I need to wait. Dan may come for me."

"OK," says Tom. "I'll just wait with you."

The snow keeps coming, but Tom and Donna talk and laugh.

"You know," says Donna, "talking with you makes me happy."

"And talking with Dan doesn't?" says Tom.

"I don't know," says Donna. "He just gets mad a lot."

"Any time you want to talk with me," says Tom, "just let me know."

"Tom," says Donna, "I have wanted to tell you — um — I don't know how to say this, but —"

"**Wait**!" Tom says. "Donna, is anyone cooking in the school?"

"Cooking!" says Donna. "No. No one is cooking!"

Tom waits. "What is it?" says Donna.

They look at the school a little longer. Then they know.

"**It's a fire**!" Tom calls out. "A **fire** in the school!"

"What do we do?" says Donna.

"I'm going in to try to put it out," says Tom.

"**Go fast**!" Donna calls out. "And I'll race over to the QT Shop to call the fire trucks and 9-1-1! Go, Tom, go!" she says. "There may not be a lot of time!"

"It's a fire!" Tom calls out. "A fire in the school!"

6. Who's Driving Donna?

"I just don't get it!" says Mrs. Newman. "The idea that anyone would light a fire in the school!"

"As for me," says Principal Walls, "I am just happy that Tom and Donna helped out by calling the fire trucks, and **fast**!"

"We raced to call for help, so the fire didn't get too big," says Tom. "A fireman from the fastest truck put it out. Others did come, but they didn't need to."

Tom, Donna, Principal Walls, and Mrs. Newman are in the hall. They are happy that the fire is out, and Mountain School is OK.

"I think it's time we go home," says Tom to Principal Walls. He and Donna walk out to his car. Donna looks at the big lot.

"You know, Tom," she says, "it's not like Dan not to be waiting for me."

"The way I see it," Tom says, "Dan lost out, and I didn't."

"Is putting out a fire your idea of a big time?" laughs Donna.

"Want me to take you home after all?" kids Tom.

"I think I'll just take you up on it!" says Donna. They get in Tom's car, laughing and talking on the way to Donna's house. There, Dan **is** waiting, and Donna does not look so happy anymore. "I need to go, Tom," she says, getting out of the car.

Tom feels a little mad that Dan is there, but he wants to hide it from Donna. "I'll see you when we work on the play next," he says as he drives off.

Donna walks over to Dan, who is waiting. "Why did he drive you home?" Dan says.

"Tom helped me out, that is all," says Donna. "It was snowing, and I did not see you anywhere."

"But maybe I was there," says Dan. "Maybe."

Donna looks at her boyfriend for a long time. She does not have any idea what he is talking about. But she knows she does not like it.

7. On the QT

"Kids, the play is on Saturday," Principal Walls says to the team that has been working on the play. "And with all the work you have put in, I think *The Lost Girl* is going to be a big hit for Mountain School!"

Jared, Kay, Jake, Donna, and Tom are laughing and talking as they go to the next class, happy with what Principal Walls has been saying.

"You know," Donna says, "the play **is** going to be a big hit! Jared and Kay, your parts are in the bag. I can tell you have worked on them a lot!"

"We have!" says Kay. "Like a fast race, but it will be over after Saturday night!"

"Keep thinking that!" says Dan, walking up to them. Then he looks at Donna. "Don't wait for me after school," he says, then walks off.

"I don't want to make you mad, Donna," says Kay, "but no one knows what to say to your boyfriend."

"What was that about, anyway?" says Jared.

Donna puts them off by saying, "Who knows?"

Wanting to help Donna, Tom says, "Why don't we forget about Dan Ringover and go to the QT Shop for something to drink after school?"

"We have to be back in class to work on the paintings for the play by 4:30," says Kay.

"That is OK," says Tom. "We can make it fast, then get back to the madhouse!"

Jared, Jake, and Kay talk, then Jared says, "You and Donna can go, Tom. We need to run home after classes. See you back in school at 4:30?"

"OK with me," says Tom, happy to get a little time with Donna.

After class, he races over to the QT, but Donna is faster. "It's not snowing anymore," she says as Tom comes in. "Do you want to get hot drinks and take them out in the sun?"

"They are on me," says Tom, who tells the QT cook what they want. Then, putting his money up and getting the hot drinks, he walks out to Donna to talk. It is a little cold, but the sun gives them a happy feeling.

"What's up with Dan?" says Tom. "You can tell me, can't you?"

"I think," says Donna, "that he knows he has lost me."

Did I hear that? Tom thinks. "Lost you?" he says.

"Dan wants me with him all the time," says Donna. "He does not want to **see** me. He wants to **own** me! And he is mad a lot. He—he takes it out on me. I can't be that bad—can I, Tom?"

"No," says Tom. "You are not bad. To me, you are like this hot drink on a cold day."

"You don't know how I needed to hear that," says Donna.

"That's OK," says Tom. "I needed to say it."

Just then, Jared races up to them. "Donna! Tom! **We need to get to the school—fast!**"

8. Put Off the Play? No Way!

"What is it?" Donna calls out, racing after Jared.

"Wait in the car!" Tom tells Donna. They get in Tom's car, make a fast stop for Jared, then ride to the school. On the way, Jared tells them what is going on.

"Mrs. Newman wanted to look over the wooden shelter for the play," says Jared. "But she walked in to see that there was graffiti paint all over the wall in back of the shelter!"

By this time, the kids are at school. They race into the hall, where Principal Walls is walking with Mrs. Newman.

"We will just have to put off the play," Mrs. Newman is saying. "I don't see any way not to."

They see Jared, and they stop talking.

"Can I see the graffiti?" Jared wants to know. "Can we see how bad it is?"

Principal Walls takes them to the wall. "There it is," he says.

"We worked so long!" Jared says. "And you tell us there will be no play?"

"You tell me," says Mrs. Newman. "Saturday is in just 3 days! How can we clean the graffiti in time?"

Jared thinks. He looks over the shelter, the wall, and the paintings for the play. "We can do it!" he says. "I know we can!"

Principal Walls and Mrs. Newman do not look like they think it can be cleaned up so fast. "I don't know," says Principal Walls. "It will take a lot of work."

"I'll help," says Donna.

"And I'll help out," says Tom.

"We will too," say Kay and Jake, walking in from the hall.

"OK, kids," says Principal Walls. "We will do what we can to keep *The Lost Girl* on for Saturday night. But it will take a lot of work."

"The play is in just 3 days! How can we clean this graffiti in time?"

"We can do it," says Jared.

"By the way," says Mrs. Newman, "do you kids have any idea who did this?"

Tom looks at Kay. Kay looks at Jake. Jake looks at Jared. And Jared looks at Donna. Donna looks at no one. Jared goes over to Mrs. Newman. "I do not know who did it, Mrs. Newman," he says, looking back at Donna, "but I **will** find out."

9. What About Donna?

Jared waits, thinking, as Principal Walls and Mrs. Newman walk off. Then he goes over to Donna and Tom, who are talking by the shelter.

"Donna," he says, "I need to talk to you."

"What about, Jared?" she says.

"About the graffiti," Jared says. "What do you know about it?"

"**Me**?" Donna calls out. "I didn't do it!"

"I didn't say that you did," Jared tells her.

"You did!" Donna says back. "And that makes me mad, Jared!"

"Wait, wait, wait!" says Tom. He wants to know who put graffiti on the play wall, but he does not want Donna to feel bad. "Jared, my man," Tom says, "this is a job for the cops, don't you think?"

"I think she knows who did it!" says Jared. "**That** is what I think!"

"And the cops will take care of it, OK?" says Tom. "Can you give me a little time to talk to her?" says Tom.

"I don't want to talk to anyone!" screams Donna. "Not you, not Jared, not **anyone**!" Then Donna takes off and races out of the school. Tom does not know what to do.

"I'm telling you, Tom," says Jared. "There was the fire the other day, and there is graffiti all over the wall we painted for the play. I **am** going to find out who did this, with or without your help."

Tom walks out of the school and into the sun. He needs to think. He likes Donna, and maybe she likes him. Who knows? But the people who are doing this to the play have to stop what they are doing!

Jared walks out in back of him. "I'm sorry," Jared says. "I know you like Donna. But a lot of people have worked on this play, Tom."

"I know."

"Are you trying to keep me from talking to Donna because you think she did it?" says Jared. "She did want the part of the Lost Girl a lot."

"No!" says Tom. "Donna did not do this. She was with me!"

"Maybe the one who likes her the most sees too little," says Jared.

Tom looks at his friend. "I see what I need to see," he tells Jared, "and I will take care of it."

"See that you do," says Jared. "And don't forget . . . I **will** find out who did this, and you may not like what I find."

Tom walks out to his car and gets in. He will drive over to Donna's house! He **has** to talk to her. He **has** to see her. But he gets there just in time to see Dan Ringover walk into the house with her. *Ringover!* he thinks. Tom stops in front of her house. *Donna, what are you doing?* he wants to know. *And what are you and Dan talking about?*

10. Cleaning Up

The next day at school, Tom does not see Donna. He knows they have to work on the play after classes to make up for lost time **and** to clean up the graffiti. It is there after school, at 4:00, that he finds her.

"I have not seen you today," he says, walking over to Donna.

"I did not want to see you," Donna tells him.

"And I think I know why," Tom says.

Donna looks at him.

"Look, Donna," says Tom, "I know Dan was with you at your house."

"**How** do you know?" Donna says.

"Because I was there," Tom comes back.

"That may be," says Donna, "but I did **not** paint the graffiti, and I did **not** light a fire in the school. What can I say?"

"That's all you have to say," says Tom. "But why did that keep you from wanting to see me today?"

"I was scared," says Donna.

"Of me?" says Tom.

"Of — of lots of people," Donna says.

"You **have** to know how I feel about you, Donna," says Tom. "Tell me you are not scared of me."

But Donna and Tom have to stop talking as Jared, Kay, Jake, and other people walk in feeling bad about the graffiti.

"Come on, kids," says Principal Walls, "it's not that bad."

"Not that bad!" the kids say.

"No," says the principal. "Look! Most of the graffiti is off the wall!"

The kids walk by the wooden shelter to look at the wall. The principal is telling it like it is! The paint is just about off the wall!

"You may have been in class," Principal Walls tells them, "but Mrs. Newman and I have been working on the wall. It's just about cleaned up!"

"OOOOOO-K!" the kids scream. "The play is back on for Saturday night!" They laugh and kid and race about, happy that the play is going to go on. "No one can stop it this time," they call out, "no one!"

"You hear that?" Jared says, looking over at Donna. "**No one.**"

11. Kay Is Next

The play is the next day! Kay and Jared know the parts of the Painter and the Lost Girl to a T, and Tom and Donna are happy as the bank teller and the cop. Jake, at times, forgets what to say as the shopkeeper, but they have all worked a lot. "Don't worry, Jake," laughs Jared, "we will help you out if you have a problem."

Jake knows that his friends — from Jared and Tom to Kay and Donna — know his part, which makes him laugh too.

"The walls are clean, the wooden shelter is painted and up," says Principal Walls, "and all you kids have to do is **not get sick**!"

Tom walks Donna out of the school. "Want to go out to dinner with me tonight?" he says. The play is the next day, and he knows she is a little scared and needs to lighten up.

"No," says Donna, "I can't."

"That was fast," says Tom. "Can you tell me why?"

"I need to — I need to talk to Dan," she says.

"You do that!" Tom says, getting mad. "Do what you want. I'm out of it."

"No, Tom!" Donna calls, but Tom has walked away, not wanting to hear what Donna has to say.

I just need to give up on Donna, Tom thinks, walking to his car. *She knows how I feel, but she wants Dan as a boyfriend, not me.*

"Jared! Jake!" Tom calls to his friends. They are getting into Jake's truck. "Want to go get dinner?" The 3 boys go to the QT Shop. Jared and Jake can tell that Tom is not happy.

"Want to talk about it?" Jared says.

"Talk about what?" says Tom.

"What do you think?" says Jared. "You and Donna!"

"There is no 'me and Donna,'" says Tom. "There is just Dan and Donna, and that is the problem. What is there to talk about?"

Tom's friends feel bad for him. "I'm OK," says Tom. "I'm just going to get a fast dinner," he says, "then go home and try to get a little sleep."

Jared looks up at Tom. He knows his friend is mad at Donna. "You say you are OK," Jared says, "but you do not look like it, Tom."

Jared and Jake know me too well, Tom thinks. And when he gets home, he finds that he does not look **or** feel OK—not at all. Sleep doesn't come fast for Tom tonight. He thinks and thinks about Donna. He thinks about Donna with Dan. And, just as it feels like he is going to sleep, his dad is getting him up.

"Tom! Tom!" Dad says. "Jared wants to talk to you."

"Jared?" says Tom. "What does he want?"

"I don't know," says Dad, "but he is not happy."

Jared walks in. "Sorry," he says to Tom and his dad. "No time to wait."

"What's up?" Tom wants to know.

"They have hit again," says Jared. "It's Kay. She's as sick as a dog."

12. The Lost Girl

"I'm on my way to Donna's," Jared says. "You call Jake."

"No way!" says Tom. "I'm going to Donna's with you."

Jared looks at Tom. "Can you take it if I find out Donna was in on the fire, the graffiti, **and** Kay getting sick?"

"I don't have to take it," Tom says. "Donna did not do it. But I **do** think she knows who did."

They get in Jared's truck and race over to Donna's. Like Tom, Donna does not look like she got a lot of sleep. He feels for her.

"What is this about?" says Donna.

"Have you talked to Kay today?" Jared says.

"I just got up," says Donna. "And no, I didn't talk to her in my sleep."

"You may be happy to know," says Jared, "that you get the part of the Lost Girl tonight after all."

"What are you talking about?" says Donna.

"It's Kay," says Tom, walking over to Donna. "She's sick."

"No! It can't be!" says Donna. She backs up. "No!" She looks at them. "You think **I** did it?"

Jared looks at her a long time. "No, Donna, I don't."

"Look," he goes on. "I like you. We have been friends for a long, long time. But I see you and Dan at school, and I see that he looks mad, and you do not look happy. I begin to think: It's not like you to light a fire or paint graffiti," Jared says, "but it **may** be like Dan."

"Can you tell us what is going on, Donna?" Tom says. "Come on. It will be OK."

Donna looks at Jared, and she looks at Tom. They are her friends, and she knows that. "I did not know that he did this to Kay," says Donna. "I am so sorry—so sorry, and I don't know what to do."

"Talk to us," says Jared, "and we can help you out."

"You say that," says Donna, "but you do not know what you are talking about."

"Is it Dan Ringover?" says Tom. "Has Ringover done all this?"

"Yes," Donna says, looking at Tom and Jared. "He did. But he did it for me."

13. Getting It Out

"Are you saying that Dan Ringover did the fire and graffiti and making Kay sick just for you?" says Jared.

"In a way. But no —," says Donna. "I'm sorry. I just don't know how to say it."

Jared comes at it in a new way. "Did you **want** him to?"

"No!" screams Donna. "You can't think that of me!"

"It's OK, Donna," says Tom. "I am here, and I know you are not like that."

Donna looks at Tom and Jared, and then at what she is wearing in the play tonight — as a bank teller. "I was happy to be in the play at all," says Donna. "But Dan is not like me. He needed me to be the Lost Girl. It was like **he** was mad because I did not get that part."

She goes on. "At the time, I did not know that Dan was the one to light the fire. But I did know that it was not like him to forget to take me home from school."

"And the graffiti?" Jared says. "What about that?"

"I just know that Dan was not happy about Kay getting the part he wanted for me. After that, he was mad."

"You know," says Tom, "Ringover didn't come to take Donna home after school the day of the fire."

"And don't forget," says Jared, "that it was the day of the graffiti painting that he was telling her not to wait for him after class."

"That's why I had to talk to him that night," says Donna.

"Which night?" says Tom.

"The night you came to my house, and Dan was there. I wanted to talk with him, to see what he was up to and if he did it."

"What did he say?" says Jared.

"He was saying he did it for me, but it was not what **I** wanted," says Donna. "It's what **he** wanted!

He got mad at me, and was saying that I was **his** girl and I have to back him up."

"Or what?" says Tom.

"Or who knows?" says Donna. "I did not want to find out."

"And when you wanted to talk to Dan, and did not go to dinner with me, what was that about?" says Tom.

"I keep telling him to keep me out of it," says Donna. "I want no part in what he is doing," she says. "I did feel like the Lost Girl, in a way. I had to tell him that I am your girl, Tom," she says, "— if you want me to be."

"**If** he wants, she says," laughs Jared. "What do you think?"

"I think that, if you feel like a Lost Girl," says Tom, "then I will make it my job to find you."

14. Tonight's the Night

Jared hears what Donna knows about Dan Ringover, then they get in Tom's truck to go see Kay. They get to her house just as Kay's dad is going to work.

"Is Kay going to be OK?" they want to know.

"She will be OK, kids," says her dad. "Go on in. Her mom can take you back to see her."

Kay does look sick, but not as sick as Jared was thinking.

"OK, what did Dan Ringover do to you?" Jared wants to know. "That is it! We're going to get him."

Kay laughs a little. "Dan may make a fire at school, and he may paint graffiti on walls," says Kay, "but he did **not** make me sick. He didn't have to. My little sister did that job on her own."

"Is Kay going to be OK?"

"I am so happy," says Donna.

They all laugh.

"No, no," Donna says, "it's just that I am happy that Dan did not do it."

"Us too," they all say.

"But he **did** make the fire and paint graffiti, and the cops will have to know," Jared tells her.

"I know that," says Donna. "I'm just happy that the school is OK, we are OK, and the play will go on."

"And, Kay," Donna says, "can I help you? I want **you** to be the Lost Girl in the play tonight. I always have."

"I think I'll be OK," says Kay. "But don't you want to be the Lost Girl?"

"No," says Donna, looking at Tom. "I feel like I have been the Lost Girl for a long time." She goes on. "Today, I just want to be the 'girl Tom finds.'"

"You can take that one to the bank," says Tom.

"That makes it a good thing that you are the bank teller after all!" kids Jared.

The Lost Girl just laughs.